Tideswell &

Guide & So

Roly Smith

**A
E**

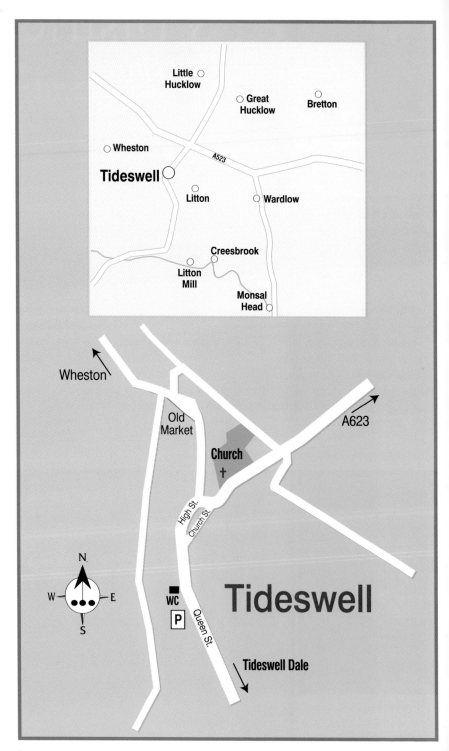

Tideswell: The Peak's 'Cathedral' Town

Tideswell (local nickname "Tidser") is a large village of ancient foundation which has the prosperous, urban air of a small town. The village gets its name from one of its earliest settlers, a Saxon called "Tidi" who first settled here in this long, dry, shallow valley above the deep gorge of the River Wye.

Tideswell is perhaps best known for its magnificent **Parish Church of St John the Baptist**, known with some justification as "the Cathedral of the Peak," and described by no less an authority than Sir John Betjeman as "a grand and inspiring church of the 14th century".

Above: The Cathedral of the Peak, details of Tideswell's Parish Church of St John the Baptist

The present 14th century Decorated style church was built on the site of an 11th century chapelry. The stately building, with its wonderfully light and airy chancel, is a rarity among Derbyshire parish churches in that it was almost entirely built within one period – in about 70 years from 1300. This gives the elegant, cruciform church a wonderful uniformity of appearance, which is missing from so many other churches. The impressive turreted and pinnacled west tower was added later, in the newly-fashionable Perpendicular style.

St John's also contains a wealth of interesting memorials, including some of the finest brasses in the Peak. Chief among these is the one to Bishop Robert Pursglove, who died in 1579, a great benefactor of the village of his birth and the founder of Tideswell's Royal Grammar School in 1560 (closed in 1927). Earlier fine brasses commemorate Sir John Foljambe (1383) and Sir Robert Lytton, of nearby Litton, who died a hundred years later. Many of the wooden furnishings in the church were carved by the local Hunstone family, who have been wood carvers of great distinction for three generations.

Brass of Sir John Foljambe
in Tideswell church

Tideswell Dale

Above and left: Cottages decorated during the "Wakes Week" festival, the old Market Place, Tideswell

The right to hold a market at Tideswell was granted to Paulinus de Bampton as early as 1251, and Edward I, "the Hammer of the Scots", stayed at Tideswell for three days in 1275 while hunting in the Royal Forest of the Peak. The hunting must have been rather successful because an order issued to Roger Lestrange, bailiff of the Peak, in August of that year, directed that "all the venison in the King's larder at Tydeswell be taken and carried to Westminster to be delivered to the keeper of the King's larder there".

At one time Tideswell held five markets a year for cattle and local produce, and those days are recalled in the name of the restored cobbled **Pot Market**, near the church. Interestingly, an old photograph taken at the turn of the 20th century shows a tethered bear in the market place, an echo of the days when bear-baiting was a popular attraction at such events.

Among a range of other interesting, mainly 18th century, buildings which grace the village, is **The George Hotel** near the church. This dates from the latter years of that century and features the then-fashionable Venetian-style louvered windows.

Tideswell has a long musical tradition, dating back to William Newton (1750-1830), a poet known as "the Minstrel of the Peak," and Samuel Slack (1737-1822) who sung before King George III. This tradition is continued by the Tideswell Male Voice Choir, the Silver Band and several smaller choirs.

Tideswell's famous well-dressings (see box opposite) are among the finest in the Peak, and take place every year on the patronal festival of St John, or "Wakes Week," in June.

Just to the south of the village, entered by a fine avenue of beech trees, is **Tideswell Dale**, a Derbyshire Wildlife Trust Nature Reserve which is noted for

Tideswell Well dressings

Tideswell's four well-dressings are among the finest in the Peak, taking place in Wakes Week at the end of June. The themes are usually ecclesiastical, and a series depicting English cathedrals is particularly well-remembered for its intricate detail and artistic excellence. The Shimwell family of Tideswell were acknowledged experts at the ancient skill, and they were responsible for re-introducing well dressing to many other Peakland villages.

Other nearby villages which have well dressings include Litton (held at the same time as Tideswell's at the end of June) and Foolow (held from the last Saturday in August). Foolow has a charming village green, complete with medieval cross and duck pond.

Above: Well dressing in Queen Street
Below: The churchyard well dressing, 2010

Cressbrook Mill

Wheston Cross

its beautiful flowers and exposures of columnar basalt rocks, which make it a geological Site of Special Scientific Interest. The large former quarry in Tideswell Dale was worked for its outcrop of hard, volcanic basalt, before being purchased and restored by the National Park Authority.

Industry came to Tideswell when the power of the nearby River Wye was harnessed for some of the first factories of the Industrial Revolution. **Cressbrook Mill** was originally built by Richard Arkwright (the inventor and manufacturing pioneer) in 1783. The present building, with its distinctive bell tower and cupola, dates from the year of the Battle of Waterloo, 1815. The mill is now converted to residential use.

The hamlet of **Wheston**, north-west of Tideswell, contains many fine 16th and 17th century houses, but is most famous for its almost complete crocketed 15th century village cross, which depicts the crucifixion.

Great & Little Hucklow

The former lead-mining village of Great Hucklow, lying beneath Hucklow Edge, was once known nationally for its outstanding amateur dramatic group the **Hucklow Players**. The group was the inspiration of Dr Laurence du Garde Peach, a well-known author, playwright and dramatist, who lived at nearby Housely and whose father was the local minister.

The Players, all of whom were local people, performed in the Unitarian Holiday

Home in the village until 1938. They then moved to a converted lead mining cupola barn which became the new playhouse. Plays were often performed in the Derbyshire dialect, which sometimes may have made them difficult to understand as audiences came from as far away as Stratford-upon-Avon and Harrogate. To aid local people, plays were often put on to coincide with the full moon, as most of the audience had to walk home to neighbouring villages after the performance. The playhouse is now used as a Scout centre for visiting groups.

Great Hucklow's Primary School was built in 1873 on a lead mine hillock – another reminder of the days when the village was a centre of the lead mining industry.

Believed to be the fifth oldest pub in England, **Ye Olde Bulls Head** in Little Hucklow claims to date back to the 12th century. It is well worth a visit to enjoy the ambience of its small downstairs rooms with open fires, collections of trinkets, tankards and mining equipment and 'the cave' up in the roof. The historic **Queen Anne Inn** in Great Hucklow is another traditional pub serving food and ales.

At Camphill Farm, high on Hucklow Edge above the village, the **Derbyshire and Lancashire Gliding Club** has its lofty headquarters, and the sight of the graceful gliders riding the thermals often fills the skies above the village. The club was one of the earliest in the country, founded in 1935 and occupies one of the most spectacular launching sites at over 1,360ft (415m) above the sea.

Also on Hucklow Edge is **The Barrel Inn**, in the parish of Bretton, which is one of the highest and oldest pubs in Derbyshire, dating from 1637. It is famous for its good food and roaring fire and enjoys spectacular views across the White Peak limestone plateau.

Left: The Old Chapel, Great Hucklow **Right:** The Barrel, Hucklow Edge

Wardlow

The dome-like detached limestone rock known as **Peter's Stone** at the northern end of **Cressbrook Dale** to the west of Wardlow marks the site of Derbyshire's last public gibbeting in 1815. The unfortunate victim was 21-year-old Anthony Lingard, who had been convicted of the murder of Hannah Oliver, the toll-keeper at **Wardlow Mires** on the main Chesterfield to Chapel-en-le-Frith road (now the A623).

William Newton, the famed "Minstrel of the Peak" was so appalled by the inhumanity of the gibbeting that he wrote a poem about it. This was to play a large part in the campaign which eventually led to the abolishment of the barbarous punishment.

Wardlow itself is a typical one-street limestone village, high on the White Peak plateau. It takes its name from the rounded hill known as **Wardlow Hay Cop** to the south, and the name is thought to mean "lookout hill." The little Gothic-style **Parish Church of the Good Shepherd** in the main street was built in 1872. Look out for the Victorian letterbox, mounted in the wall near **Manor Farm**, also in the main street.

Miller's Dale

The presence of the two cast iron railway bridges which now carry the **Monsal Trail** give the only clue to this tiny hamlet's former importance.

When the Midland Line (see box) was constructed in the 1860s it followed the Valley of the River Wye through some of the most difficult country in Britain. Miller's Dale became the junction for the fast-expanding spa town of Buxton. Some of the railwaymens' cottages still survive down by the river. The former station has been converted to a Ranger Briefing Centre and car park by the National Park Authority.

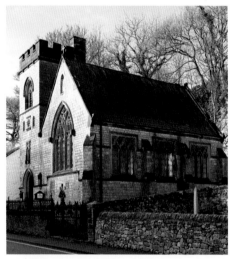
Parish Church of St Anne, Miller's Dale

Also by the river is the 19th century former corn mill, now a private house, which gave the hamlet its name. The **Parish Church of St Anne** was built in 1880 in the Victorian Gothic style by Canon Samuel Andrew of nearby Tideswell. The railway closed in 1968 and was converted to the Monsal Trail walking and riding route (see box p.14).

Parts of the line, including a former limestone quarry down the line from the station, are now managed by the Derbyshire Wildlife Trust as a nature reserve. The monumental lime kilns just down the line from the station, which emptied

Peter's Stone, Cressbrook Dale

their products straight into railway wagons beneath, have been restored to their former condition. Lime was an important local commodity for many years, and the presence of the railway made its export easy. Upstream along the trail are the tremendous limestone buttresses of Chee Dale, a favourite haunt of rock climbers.

Monsal Head and the River Wye

Monsal Head

Monsal Head is one of the most popular viewpoints in the Peak District and the view from the car park outside the Monsal Head Hotel is justly famous. It takes in a sweeping horse-shoe bend of the River Wye. The Iron Age hill-fort on the summit of Fin Cop is prominent to the west above the five-arched viaduct. This once carried Midland Line trains between London and Manchester and is now the Monsal Trail. To the north west, the Wye runs towards Upperdale and Cressbrook.

In the summer of 2009, Longstone Local History Group conducted a three-week archaeological investigation of Fin Cop to try to find out how and when the ramparts of the hill-fort were built, as well as discovering more about the people who had occupied the site.

The most surprising result was the discovery of a skeleton of a human body as the stone and earth rubble was being cleared from the hill-fort ditch. It seemed that, during the destruction of the ramparts, the human corpse of a young woman was thrown into the ditch along with the fort wall material.

The construction of the Monsal Dale or Headstone viaduct and the Midland line through the unspoiled valley of the Wye, in the 1860s, attracted a famously-ferocious outburst from the Victorian conservationist and critic John Ruskin. Writing in *Fors Clavigera – Letters to the Workmen and Labourers of Great Britain* in 1896 he fumed:

A weir in Monsal Dale

There was a rocky valley between Buxton and Bakewell, once upon a time, divine as the Vale of Tempe; you might have seen the Gods there morning and evening – Apollo and all the sweet Muses of the light – walking in fair procession on the lawns of it, and to and fro among the pinnacles of its crags. You cared neither for Gods nor grass, but for cash (which you did not know the way to get); you thought you could get it by what the *Times* calls "Railroad Enterprise." You Enterprised a Railroad through the valley – you blasted its rocks away, heaped thousands of tons of shale into its lovely stream. The valley is gone, and the Gods with it; and now, every fool in Buxton can be at Bakewell in half an hour, and every fool in Bakewell at Buxton; which you think a lucrative process of exchange – you Fools Everywhere.

Times change, and now the 300 feet (91 m) long Headstone viaduct, some 40 feet (12m) above the river, is a protected structure on the Monsal Trail.

Litton

The Midland Line and Monsal Trail

The construction of the Midland line through the difficult hill country of the Peak was a triumph of optimism and Victorian railway engineering. The Manchester, Buxton, Matlock and Midlands Junction Railway reached Rowsley in 1849, before the money ran out, and it was amalgamated with the Midland Railway which was aiming to link London and Manchester.

The Duke of Devonshire refused permission for the line to pass through his park at Chatsworth, so an alternative route was planned up the Wye Valley to Miller's Dale. The Duke of Rutland would only allow passage of the railway through his grounds at Haddon via a 'cut-and-cover' tunnel. This was constructed only after an initial tragic collapse which resulted in the deaths of four men in March, 1861.

The Miller's Dale junction served as the branch line to the popular spa town of Buxton. The main line continued north through the Peak Forest tunnel and down to Chapel-en-le-Frith via the Dove Holes tunnel, 1 mile 1,224 yards in length, the longest on the line.

The enormously expensive line, which required seven tunnels, two major viaducts (at Monsal Head and Chee Dale) and 11 other bridges in only five and a half miles, was eventually completed and opened in May, 1863.

Beeching's axe

The line closed under the axe of Beeching in 1968, and was bought by the Peak District National Park Authority. It was converted to the Monsal Trail walking, riding and cycling route. All the tunnels were closed for safety reasons, and routes diverted around them. There are long-term plans by Peak Rail Ltd to re-open the line for steam trains between Matlock and Buxton.

In November, 2009, it was announced that four of the old railway tunnels would be re-opened as part of a £3.79m new cycle trail across the Peak District National Park between Matlock and Buxton.

The Department of Transport announced a £1m contribution towards the proposed Buxton to Bakewell section. This would include re-opening four 437 yard/400m tunnels for cyclists, walkers and horse-riders on the Monsal Trail. It would mean that visitors could arrive by train and cycle into the heart of the national park, or that residents could cycle to the station to commute into nearby cities.

Cycling England has already pledged £1.25m to the project. It chose the Peak District to pilot extending its innovative Cycling Towns and Cities concept because 32 per cent of the UK population lives within 60 miles of the district, which already has a 58-mile network of cycle trails and cycle-hire centres.

The plan would also link up existing cycle trails along the former railway routes of the Monsal, High Peak and Tissington Trails. The national park's 'capital' of Bakewell and outlying villages would have designated cycling routes to access the trails.

Litton

In many ways Litton, a small village 1,000ft (300m) up on the limestone plateau, is a typical White Peak village. Clustered around its long village green with an ancient cross at one end, the range of stone-built cottages, mainly dating from the 17th and 18th centuries, is as pretty as a picture, and as a result, much-photographed.

The **Red Lion public house** is a popular hostelry in the centre of the village, where the stocks still stand on the green. Much of Litton's prosperity was built on the traditional dual industries of lead-mining and farming, of which only farming now remains as an important employer of local labour.

The combined **School, Church and Library** was built by Canon Samuel Andrews. He was the vicar of nearby Tideswell, in 1865. A more modern church was built in 1929.

One of Litton's most famous sons was William Bagshawe, the so-called "Apostle of the Peak," who was an outstanding nonconformist preacher in this land of non-conformism. He is buried at Chapel-en-le-Frith.

Down in the dale is the notorious **Litton Mill**, built in 1782. Here the mill-owner Ellis Needham inflicted some of the worst examples of the exploitation of child labour among his young apprentices. Many had been sent to Litton from the workhouses of London. The story of one of their number, Robert Blincoe, was told in John Brown's *A Memoir of Robert Blincoe* published in 1832 – a document which did much to change the cruel and antiquated laws covering child labour. The mill is now converted to housing.

Litton hosts a popular well-dressing in June each year.

Litton Mill

FURTHER INFORMATION

Accommodation

Lists of various types of accommodation can be obtained from the Tourist Information Centre. There is a full range of serviced accommodation, including hotels, guest houses, bed and breakfasts, farm houses, a youth hostel at Eyam (☎ 0845 371 9738) and camping and caravan sites.

Tourist Information Centre

Bakewell Visitor Centre
The Old Market Hall, Bridge Street, Bakewell, Derbyshire DE45 1DS
☎ 01629 816558; www.peakdistrict.gov.uk; open daily

Car parking

In Cherry Tree Square, Tideswell.

Doctors

Tideswell Surgery
Parke Road, Tideswell SK17 8NS ☎ 01298 871292.

Attractions

Derbyshire and Lancashire Gliding Club
Camphill, Great Hucklow, Buxton, Derbyshire SK17 8RQ
☎ 01298 871270; www.dlgc.org.uk; visits and flights by appointment only.

Eyam Hall
Eyam, Hope Valley, Derbyshire S32 5QW
☎ 01433 631976; www.eyamhall.co.uk

Eyam Museum
Hawkhill Road, Eyam, Hope Valley, Derbyshire S32 5QP
☎ 01433 631371; www.eyam.org.uk

Published by **Ashbourne Editions**
Moor Farm Road West, Ashbourne, Derbyshire DE6 1HD
Tel: (01335) 347349 Fax: (01335) 347303

1st edition: ISBN: 978-1-873-775-37-0

© **Roly Smith 2011**

Print
Gomer Press, Llandysul, Wales

Design
Mark Titterton – www.ceibagraphics.co.uk

Photography
© Mark Titterton

Front Cover: "The Cathedral of the Peak – Tideswell Church **Back cover top (l-r):** Monsal Dale Viaduct, wooden sculpture – Tideswell Dale, Litton **Back cover main:** Tideswell **Page 1:** Monsal Dale viewed from Monsal Head